Vac[illegible] from London

Written by Philippa Werry

Illustrated by Spike Wademan

Characters

Mrs Morris	**Teacher**
Brian	**Rita**
Norma	**Pat**

Norma: I want to go home, Rita.

Rita: Don't say that, Norma.

Norma: But I do want to. I don't want to be on this train.

Rita: Remember what Mum said when she said goodbye to us. "Be brave and don't **complain**."

Norma: And she said that you had to look after me.

Rita: Don't worry Norma, I will.

Brian: It was scary at the railway station. There must have been hundreds of us.

Teacher: That's because there *are* hundreds of other children just like you being sent to live in the countryside.

Norma: It was horrible at the railway station.

Brian: You were crying.

Rita: Don't be mean, Brian. She's only six. She's never been away from home before.

Teacher: It will be a big adventure, Norma. You'll have a lovely time.

Brian: I'm sure you'll like the countryside, Norma.

Teacher: I've always loved the tall, thick **hedgerows** that line the narrow country roads. You'll see lots of animals too, like rabbits and badgers in the fields.

Norma: Badgers?

Teacher: We should be there very soon. Have you all still got your labels pinned on?

Rita: I've got mine. Rita Smith, Green Wood School, North London.

Brian: The train's slowing.

Norma (*almost crying*):
Where are we, Rita?

Teacher: All right children, we're getting off here. Stay close to me, please.

Brian: Look Norma, it really is the countryside. Look at those cows... and the sheep in that field over there.

Norma: It smells funny.

Brian: No, it just smells different from the city.

Mrs Morris: Hello there. Are you the children from Green Wood School?

Teacher: That's right.

Mrs Morris: I'm Mrs Morris, the **billeting officer**. We're going to walk over to the village hall and find out who you're going to be staying with.

Rita (*to herself*):
I hope we get someone nice.

Mrs Morris: Have you all still got your labels? And your **gas masks**?

Rita: Please, Mrs Morris, why do we need these? We won't be **bombed** out here in the countryside, will we?

Brian: My dad said that's why we're being sent away, in case they bomb London.

Teacher: Nobody knows what's going to happen.

Norma: Rita, I want to go home.

Rita: We'll be able to stay together, won't we, Mrs Morris?

Mrs Morris: We'll try and keep you together, but it depends on who wants to take you.

Norma (*crying*):
I don't want to be on my own!

Brian (*whispering*):
Look, those children over there are watching us.

Rita: That must be the village school. And look, a real **village green** – with ducks on it!

Pat: You're the vaccies, aren't you?

Brian: Who?

Pat: The **evacuees** from London. Why have you got those funny labels on?

Rita: We have to wear them, in case we get lost.

Pat: Where are all your things?

Brian: We were only allowed one bag each, and our gas mask, and our lunch for the train.

Pat:	She's got a doll.
Rita:	She's allowed. It's her favourite toy.
Pat:	I'm Pat. So what's it like up in London?
Norma:	London's wonderful. There are double-decker buses and lots of museums and shops – it's much better than...
Rita:	Norma! Ssh!
Pat:	My dad says London's horrible. He says it's all dirty and smelly.
Brian:	It is not!
Pat:	And he says London's going to get it when the bombs start...
Brian:	Anyway, it smells down here, too.

Teacher:	That's a good healthy country smell. You'll soon get used to it.
Norma:	I don't want to get used to it. I want to go back to...
Mrs Morris:	Over here, children. Now, some of you have already been **allocated** homes. The rest of you will have to wait here and we'll see who wants to take you.
Pat:	You're coming to our school.
Rita:	Are we?
Pat:	Our teacher says it's going to be a real squash with all of you here. She says we might have to divide into morning and afternoon school.

Mrs Morris: Brian – those people over there want a strong, **capable** boy to go and help them on their farm. Would you like that?

Brian: A real farm, with tractors?

Mrs Morris: That's right.

Brian: That would be great!

Teacher: You're very lucky, Brian. Fancy living on a farm! Say goodbye to your friends, then.

Mrs Morris: Off you go, Brian. They're waiting for you.

Norma: What if no one wants us, Rita?

Pat: Someone will, I'm sure.

Norma: But everyone else has gone. We're the last ones.

Pat: I'm glad I'm not an evacuee. I'd hate to have to leave *my* home.

Rita: Is your family going to take any evacuees?

Pat: We've got two already. My mum says that's quite **sufficient**.

SCHOOL

Mrs Morris: Two girls? Yes, I've got two girls over here. Rita, Norma, this is Miss Allonby. She lives in a nice little cottage overlooking the village green.

Norma: Can we go and feed the ducks on the pond?

Pat: I'm sure Miss Allonby will let you do that. She's really nice. She's my great aunt.

Teacher: Off you go then, Rita. Take your sister. You girls are very lucky. Don't forget to write to your mother and tell her where you are.